# Miniature Dogs

by Alix Wood

WINDMILL BOOKS

New York

Published in 2017 by **Windmill Books**, An Imprint of Rosen Publishing
29 East 21st Street, New York, NY 10010

Editor: Eloise Macgregor
Designer: Alix Wood

Photo Credits: Cover, 1, 4, 5, 7, 8 right, 9, 10, 12, 13, 14, 15, 16, 17, 18, 19, 21, 22, 23, 24, 26, 27 bottom, 29 © AdobeStock; 6 © Pushkin Museum; 8 left © Shutterstock; 11 © Dreamstime; 20 © iStock; 25 © supportdogs.org.uk; 27 top © angela n; 28 © John Trethorne

Cataloging-in-Publication Data
Names: Wood, Alix.
Title: Miniature dogs / Alix Wood.
Description: New York : Windmill Books, 2017. | Series: Mini animals| Includes index.
Identifiers: ISBN 9781499481587 (pbk.) | ISBN 9781499481594 (library bound) | ISBN 9781508192978 (6 pack)
Subjects: LCSH: Dogs--Juvenile literature. | Dogs--Size--Juvenile literature.
Classification: LCC SF426.5 W66 2017 | DDC 636.76--dc23

Manufactured in the United States of America
CPSIA Compliance Information: Batch #: BW17PK. For Further Information contact: Windmill Books, New York, New York at 1-866-478-0556

# Contents

# Cute Tiny Dogs

All dogs originally came from one type of gray wolf. Now, dogs come in all shapes and sizes. This is because, over time, people have **bred** dogs to be good at different things.

People wanted dogs to help them hunt, or herd animals, or use as guard dogs. To breed hunting dogs, people would only breed select dogs that had a great sense of smell and liked to chase. Gradually, over generations, all their dogs would be good hunters.

If people wanted to hunt rabbits a small dog was ideal. It could fit down a rabbit hole and chase the rabbit out.

4

Dogs are put into groups at dog shows depending on their type. Groups include herding dogs, terriers, toy dogs, or working dogs. Many small dogs are in the toy group, even if they are also terriers or working dogs.

## Cute Alert!

Sometimes the same breed of dog is bred to different sizes, like this standard and miniature poodle (right).

# Why Breed Small Dogs?

People love miniature dogs. One reason is simply because they are really cute! Their small size means that they can be taken just about anywhere. They don't eat much food or need much exercise.

Small dogs were kept as **status symbols**, as the pets were a luxury and had no particular job to do. Some dogs did serve a purpose, though. Their owners were said to have kept them to attract **fleas** away from themselves!

In Europe in the 18th and 19th century tiny dogs were very fashionable. In this painting a Russian princess is pictured with her pet pug.

## Cute Alert!

Some people love to take their dog wherever they go. This is much easier if your dog fits in your purse!

A dog shouldn't be thought of as a **fashion accessory**. Small dogs can live for up to 20 years. Owners must be sure they can give a dog a good home for many years before they decide to keep one as a pet.

# Tiny Chihuahuas

The Chihuahua is the world's smallest breed of dog. An adult Chihuahua usually weighs between 3-6 pounds (1.4-2.7 kg). Chihuahuas measure around 6-9 inches (15-23 cm) tall at the shoulder. These tiny dogs have a big personality, though!

Chihuahuas come from Chihuahua, Mexico. Visitors to Mexico would bring the little dogs home with them. They are now one of the most popular dogs in the US.

NORTH
AMERICA

Chihuahua

MEXICO

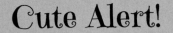

## Cute Alert!

Chihuahuas shiver when cold, excited, or scared. A sweater can help keep them warm when outdoors in cold or wet weather.

Surprisingly, tiny Chihuahuas make great watchdogs! They have a fierce bark and form close bonds with their owners. In 2011 in California, a Chihuahua named Paco chased two armed robbers from his owner's store!

Despite their bravery, it's not a good idea to leave a Chihuahua on its own in the yard. Being so small, it could be attacked by a hawk, large dog, or coyote.

# The Perfect Lapdogs

A lapdog can be any breed of dog that is small enough to lie comfortably on its owner's lap, and lazy enough to want to. Pugs have been popular lapdogs for hundreds of years. Several European royal families had pet pugs. In 1572, a pug named Pompey saved the life of a Dutch prince by waking him when murderers crept into his tent.

**Cute Alert!**
Pugs make good lapdogs. Most pugs like nothing better than lazing around with their owner.

As most pugs are naturally lazy, some pug owners take their pet out in a stroller. That way, the pug can get a ride home when it gets tired.

Pug puppies, like all puppies, can be full of energy. As pugs get older they tend to get lazier. Because of their short noses pugs don't breathe very easily. They find it hard to do too much exercise, particularly in hot weather.

11

# Little Hunting Terriers

Yorkshire terriers, or "Yorkies," were originally bred to catch rats in the mines and mills of Yorkshire, England. Yorkies were later used to hunt animals much larger than themselves, such as foxes and badgers.

## Cute Alert!

Most adult Yorkies weigh no more than 7 pounds (3.2 kg), the same as a tiny newborn baby.

Hunters would carry the Yorkies in their pockets! Tiny Yorkies became well known for their bravery when faced with a cornered, angry badger in its den.

Although Chihuahuas are the smallest breed of dog, a Yorkshire terrier named Sylvia is the shortest dog on record. She was just 2.5 inches (6.3 cm) tall and weighed 4 ounces (113 g)! She lived for just two years. Unusually small dogs often have health problems.

a cute Yorkie puppy

Yorkies were used by **poachers** to hunt rabbits. Poachers found the Yorkie's long hair useful. They would use it to pull the dog and its catch out of a hole, or quickly grab the dog as they ran away from the law!

# Caring for a Miniature Dog

Tiny dogs need some care to keep them happy and healthy. Even the smallest dogs need exercise. Walking keeps them fit and all dogs love to explore. Dogs like to play fetch or chase a ball around. Ideally even a small dog should have a yard to play in.

It's important to get a young dog used to different places, people, and animals. This will help them be calm in new situations.

14

# Dog Grooming

Some dog care such as clipping the coat and nails is best done by a professional groomer. Owners must do regular routine grooming themselves, too, though.

1. Little dogs can find bathtime stressful. A squeaky toy can help keep them busy. Make sure the water is not too hot or cold and use a special dog shampoo.

2. Wrap the dog in a warm towel once they are out of the water, to keep it from getting cold.

3. Groom your dog at least once a week. Brush from nose to tail with a soft brush.

4. Small dogs often have problems with tooth decay. Brush their teeth once or twice a week to help prevent this. You can get special meaty-flavored dog toothpaste!

# Teaching Dogs Tricks

One of the great things about dogs is that people can train them to understand some commands. Most dogs will learn commands such as "sit," "lie down," and "come."

Dog training works best when owners reward a dog when it does well, rather than scold it when it does badly. **Housebreaking** a dog takes a lot of patience. Owners need to watch for signs that the dog needs to go to the bathroom and then get them outside quickly!

clicker

This little poodle is learning the command "come." Some owners use a clicker to help train their dog. They reward with a treat while clicking the clicker. Soon the dog will not need the treat and work just for the reward of a click.

If a dog becomes really good at learning commands, it may be a good idea to enter **agility** competitions. Dog agility is a sport where a **handler** directs their dog through an obstacle course. It is a race against time. Dogs run off leash and the handler can only control the dog using their voice, or hand and body signals.

Toy poodles are very good at agility. Jumps are adjusted depending on the height of the dog, so small dogs can still compete. They can be better than larger dogs at tackling obstacles like the A-frame, below.

## Cute Alert!

Poodles are intelligent and easy to train. They are also great for people who are **allergic** to dog hair, as they don't shed their coats.

17

# The Trouble with Teacups

Unusually small dogs are sometimes known as "teacup" dogs. They can be any breed of small dog. Although they are cute, most good dog breeders will not breed undersized dogs. The dogs are usually unhealthy and bred by people who don't have the dog's best interests at heart.

## Cute Alert!

Teacup dogs were given the name because they were small enough to fit inside a teacup. Very small puppies used to be called "**runts**."

18

The fashion for very small dogs has led to some people breeding teacup dogs purely for money. Breeding very small dogs can create health problems. A small female dog can struggle to give birth to her puppies. Teacup dogs may suffer from heart problems and other serious illnesses, too.

Some breeders may lie and say their puppies are older than they are, so they appear to be teacup dogs. Even runts will usually eventually grow to be full-sized dogs.

The best way to tell how big a puppy will grow is to meet the puppy's parents.

# Wo. king Miniatu. e Dogs

Most terriers were at one time used for hunting. Terriers can hunt rats, rabbits, foxes, raccoons, opossums, and badgers. The Jack Russell terrier is one of the most successful little hunting dogs.

The Jack Russell's narrow chest size means it can fit into small burrows and still turn around. If a dog has to dig to make a tunnel wider, he can get trapped in the tunnel by the dirt piled behind him. Hunters carry a shovel, in case they have to dig the dog out again!

Jack Russells love to dig. Be warned — they will dig up their owner's yard, and they are great at escaping from it, too!

## Cute Alert!

Jack Russells have plenty of energy. They will play fetch for as long as their owner wants to!

Jack Russells are very intelligent. However, they are **strong-willed**, so they can be difficult to train. The little dogs are friendly toward people. They will chase cats, and can be quite **aggressive** with other dogs. Jack Russells are fearless, so they will often pick fights with dogs that are much bigger than themselves! They are best suited to an energetic family with a strong yard fence and firm, friendly discipline.

# Sausage Dog Dachshunds

The dachshund is a short-legged, long-bodied hound. Hounds are bred to follow a scent. Dachshunds come in three different types of coat: smooth, long-haired, and wire-haired. They also come in either standard or miniature size. They can be several different colors, too.

**Cute Alert!**
The dachshund has been described as being half a dog high, and a dog and a half long!

standard long-haired dachshund

miniature smooth-coated dachshund

standard wire-haired dachshund

Some racetracks hold dachshund races. Though fun to watch, dachshunds often get bad backs, and should not be forced to run.

Miniature dachshunds are only 5-7 inches (13-18 cm) tall. A standard dachshund is 8-11 inches (20-27 cm) tall. The dogs originally came from Germany. They were used to hunt badgers. "Dachs" is German for badger, so their name in German means "badger hound." They were bred to have short legs so they could fit into badger dens.

Dachshunds are bred to burrow, so they love to snuggle under the covers.

# Tiny Helpful Dogs

Most people have seen large Labrador Retrievers working as **guide dogs**. Miniature dogs help people, too. They are often used to visit hospitals to cheer up patients. Their small size can be an advantage. They can be easily lifted into hospital beds or onto wheelchairs. They can be held more easily than larger dogs, too.

Some little dogs can be trained to sense if their owner is about to have a **seizure**. Other dogs act as companions for people with **anxiety** or **autism**.

Little dogs can be trained to help deaf people. The dogs are trained to alert their owner to sounds such as doorbells, smoke alarms, and alarm clocks.

Billy the Jack Russell (right) makes his disabled owner's life better. He fetches help if she collapses. He helps her get dressed and undressed, answers the door to visitors, and helps pick up anything she drops. He can turn on lights and open doors. He has been trained to make his work seem like a game, so he really enjoys his job!

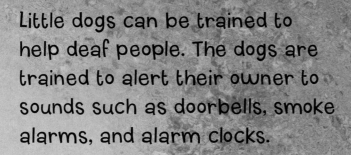

## Cute Alert!

A smaller **support dog** is much easier to house and cheaper to feed than a large breed. They are easier to take everywhere, too.

# Dog Shows Are Fun

Entering a dog show can be fun. There are different classes for different breeds of dog. Most miniature dogs are entered into the toy or terrier classes. Dogs are judged on whether they are good examples of their breed. Before a dog show, owners often get their dogs used to being handled by strangers. Then it's not such a surprise when the judge approaches them!

## Cute Alert!

Owners spend a lot of time getting their dogs ready for a dog show. This young Shih Tzu is having his ears brushed.

Little dogs can also enter agility or obedience competitions. Terriers or dachshunds can enter competitions to show off their hunting skills. Children can take part in junior handler classes to show off their dog-handling skills, too.

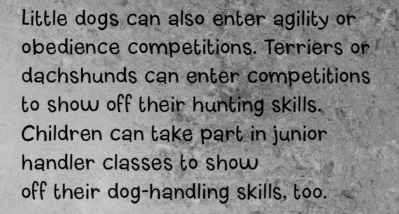

Waiting their turn at the dog show

Some dog shows have other fun contests. Some have "best rescue dog" classes, or "waggiest tail." This girl and her Chihuahua are entering a fancy dress competition.

# Test Your Knowledge

1 Why are small dogs good at hunting rabbits?
a) they look a little like a rabbit
b) they easily fit down rabbit holes
c) they run faster than big dogs

2 What is the smallest breed of dog?
a) the chihuahua
b) the pug
c) the Labrador

3 What do some dog trainers
use a clicker for?
a) to reward the dog when
it has done well
b) to get a dog used to
odd noises
c) to count how many times
a dog has been good

4 Teacup dogs can often be unhealthy.
a) true  b) false

**5** What is a lapdog?
a) a dog that likes to run fast
b) a dog that loves the water
c) a dog that likes to sit on laps

**6** Which type of dog is often used for hunting?
a) lapdogs  b) terriers  c) toy dogs

**7** What do dogs do in an agility competition?
a) dance
b) hunt
c) go through an obstacle course

**8** What does the German word "dachshund" mean?
a) badger hound
b) sausage dog
c) long dog

# Glossary

**aggressive** Showing readiness to attack.

**agility** A dog sport in which a handler directs a dog through an obstacle course.

**allergic** Having a reaction to something caused by an allergy.

**anxiety** Fearfulness.

**autism** A disorder where people have problems interacting and communicating with other people.

**bred** Raised animals for their young.

**fashion accessory** A decorative item that goes with one's clothes.

**fleas** Small wingless bloodsucking insects.

**guide dogs** Dogs that have been trained to lead a blind person.

**handler** A person who trains or has charge of an animal.

**housebreaking** Training a pet to go to the bathroom outside the house.

**poachers** People who hunt or fish illegally.

**runts** The smallest in a litter of animals.

**seizure** A sudden attack of illness or a fit.

**status symbols** A possession taken to indicate a person's wealth or status.

**strong-willed** Determined to do as one wants.

**support dog** A dog that is trained to help people with disabilities.

# Further Information

## Books

Bozzo, Linda. *I Like Chihuahuas! (Discover Dogs with the American Canine Association)*. New York, NY: Enslow Publishing, 2016.

Bozzo, Linda. *I Like Pugs! (Discover Dogs with the American Canine Association)*. Berkeley Heights, NJ: Enslow Elementary, 2012.

Morey, Allan. *Yorkshire Terriers (Tiny Dogs)*. North Mankato, MN: Capstone Press, 2016.

## Websites

For web resources related to the subject of this book, go to: **www.windmillbooks.com/weblinks** and select this book's title.

# Index

Answers 1) b, 2) a, 3) a, 4) a, 5) c, 6) b, 7) c, 8) a